THE GOLDEN BOOK OF
WORDS

by Selma Lola Chambers

illustrated by Louis Cary

 **GOLDEN PRESS**

Western Publishing Company, Inc.
® Racine, Wisconsin

INTRODUCTION

It is fascinating for very young children to associate a word with its pictorial representation.

In THE GOLDEN BOOK OF WORDS, each small picture represents a specific word. The pictures are arranged in groups—The Family, Things That Grow, Things That Go, Numbers, and so forth. Children will enjoy finding pictures of familiar objects and activities.

THE GOLDEN BOOK OF WORDS is intended for use by children who are just learning to read. They will soon begin to associate the written symbols with the pictures.

This book offers many opportunities for games of word recognition and spelling. If left to the spontaneous use of young children, it is likely to lead to a great variety of activities.

Third Printing, 1974

Library of Congress Cataloging in Publication Data
Chambers, Selma Lola, 1908-
    The golden book of words.

    Editions published in 1948-1955 under title: The little golden book of words.
    SUMMARY: Appropriate illustrations accompany words, such as boy—girl, swim—walk, one—two, which are arranged into such inclusive groups as People, Things We Do, and Numbers.
    1. Primers—1950- 2. English language—Glossaries, vocabularies, etc.—Juvenile literature. (1. Primers. 2. Vocabulary) I. Cary, Louis F., 1915- illus. II. Title.
PE1119.C45 1974 428'.1 73-12078
ISBN 0-307-10497-4 ISBN 0-307-60497-7 (lib. bdg.)

The Family

grandfather

father

mother

grandmother

brother

baby

sister

People

he

she

man

woman

children

they.

girl

boy

More People

postman

neighbor

fireman

policewoman

teacher

ice-cream man

friends

Colors

purple

red

black

yellow

blue

orange

brown

green

pink

gray

white

Things to Play With

horn

balloon

jump rope

sled

truck

drum

teddy bear

kite

wagon

doll

ball

puzzle

train

blocks

marbles

roller skates

tricycle

Clothes

earmuffs

skirt

shirt

snowsuit

pajamas

rubbers

mittens

socks

slippers

boots

suit

overalls

hat

shoes

coat

dress

underwear

sweater

pants

gloves

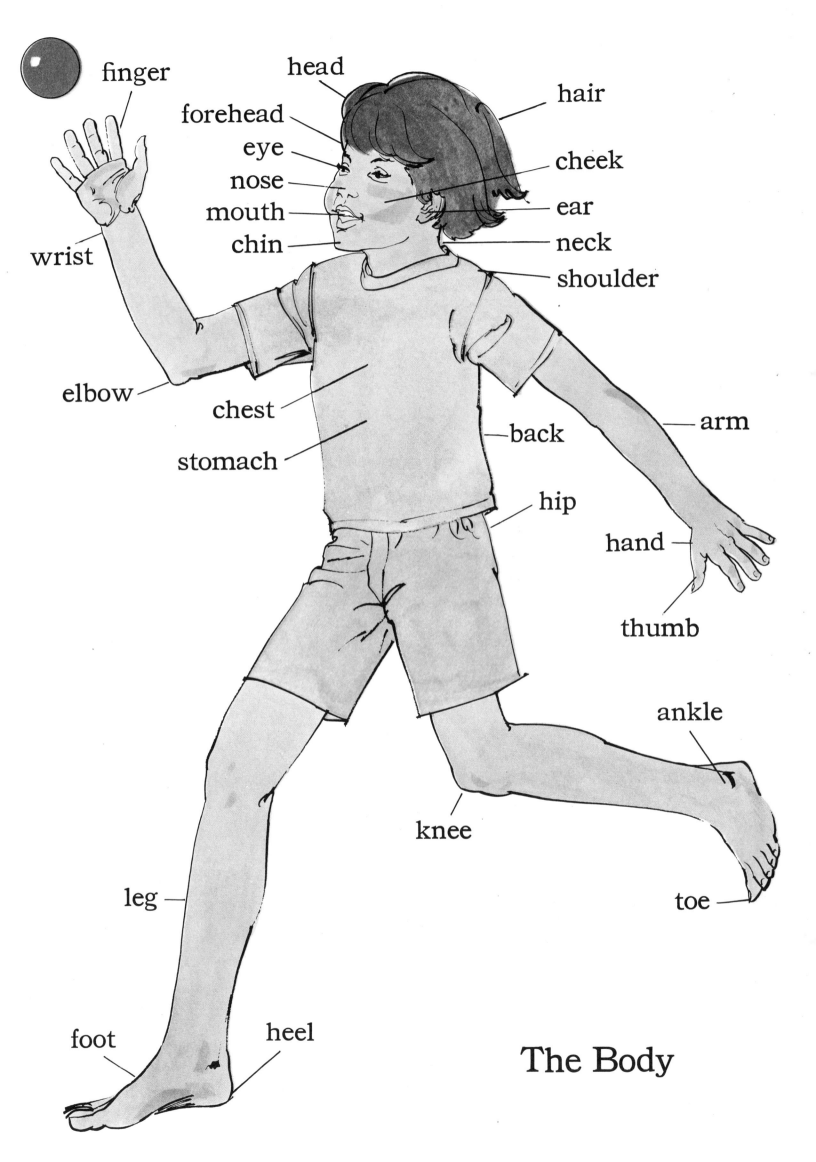

finger

head

hair

forehead

cheek

eye

nose

ear

mouth

chin

neck

shoulder

wrist

elbow

chest

back

stomach

arm

hip

hand

thumb

ankle

knee

leg

toe

foot

heel

The Body

Things to Eat

eggs

carrot

apple

milk

cake

orange

cheese

potato

corn

jelly

celery

tomato

grapefruit

peach

candy

banana

cookies

meat

lettuce

bread and butter

grapes

pear

ice cream

pancakes

Things That Grow

tree

strawberry

flower

bush

weed

tree

corn

fern

vine

grass

Things We Do

jump

write

dance

work

build

run

swing

walk

swim

read

draw

blow

crawl

sleep

eat

spoon

glass

Things
We Use

pan

dishes

scissors

paper

knife

fork

table

broom

chair

iron

clock

crayons

comb

pencil

hairbrush

toothbrush

soap

radio

paintbrush

book

telephone

paints

box

television

towel

Things That Go

rocket

airplane

tractor

taxi

car

truck

trailer truck

motorboat

fire engine

bus

helicopter

train

steamship

Places to Go

home

movies

beach

park

school

country

yard

museum

city

store

friend's house

zoo

church

Zoo Animals

bear

fox

giraffe

monkey

deer

lion

elephant

hippopotamus

turtle

snake

Farm Animals

goat

horse

sheep

cat

cow

pig

dog

Birds

hen

owl

parrot

robin

duck

turkey

pigeon

crow

sparrow

eagle

canary

Word Helpers

to the store

from the store

stop

go

in the house

out
of the house

over the fence

under the fence

empty

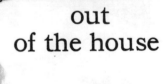

full

up the stairs

down the stairs

socks on

socks off

raining

not raining

before
the haircut

after the haircut

many fish

few fish

old shoes

new shoes

Shapes and Sizes

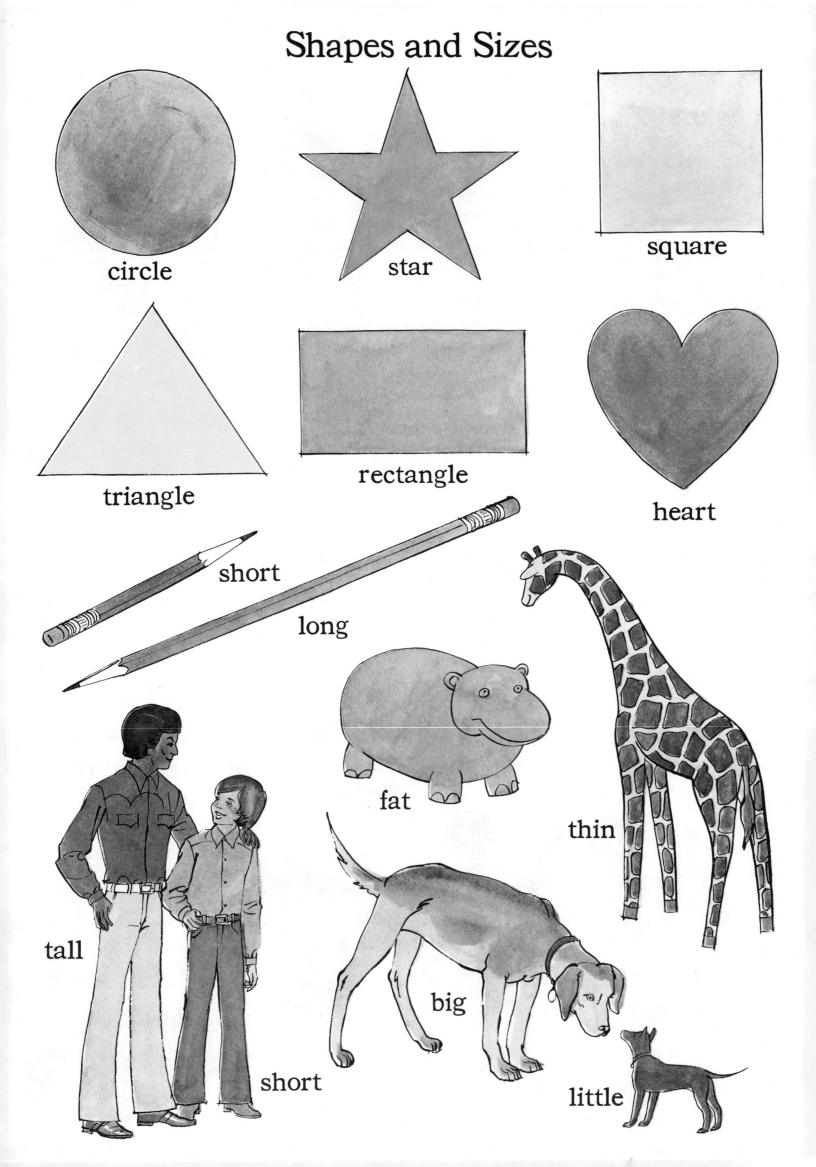

circle

star

square

triangle

rectangle

heart

short

long

fat

thin

tall

short

big

little